The Great Songbook of Nursery RHYMES

duviPlay

Collection compiled and transcribed by Tomeu Alcover
© Duviplay Music Publishing. 2017
www.duviplay.com
ISBN-13: 978-1977963406
ISBN-10: 1977963404

CONTENTS

Brother John

French nursery rhyme

Are you sleep-ing? Are you sleep-ing? Broth-er John.

Broth - er John. Morn ing bells are ring - ing,

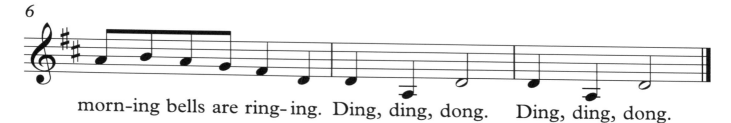

morn-ing bells are ring-ing. Ding, ding, dong. Ding, ding, dong.

D
Are you sleeping?
Are you sleeping?
Brother John.
Brother John.
Morning bells are ringing,
morning bells are ringing.
Ding, ding, dong. Ding, ding, dong.

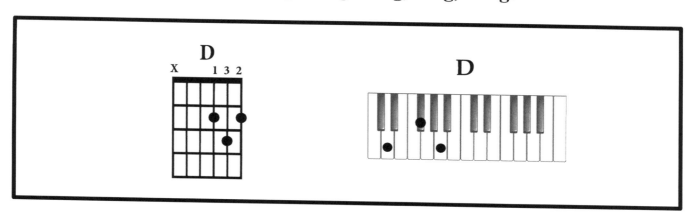

Little Bo Peep

English nursery rhyme

Lit-tle Bo-Peep has lost her sheep and does - n't know to find them. Leave them a - lone and they'll come home, wag - ging their ta - ils be - hind them.

C   G7
Little Bo-Peep has lost her sheep
C   G7
and doesn't know where to find them.
C   G7
Leave them alone and they'll come home,
C   G7 C
wagging their tails behind them.

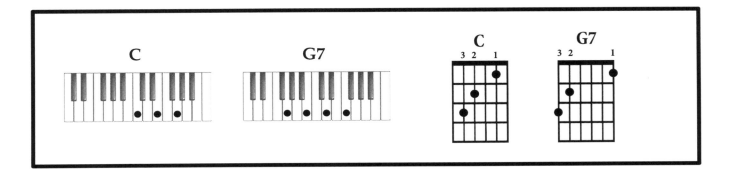

Bobby Shafto's Gone to Sea

English nursery rhyme

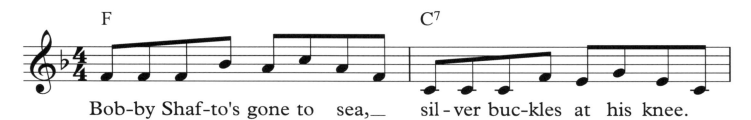

Bob-by Shaf-to's gone to sea,__ sil-ver buc-kles at his knee.

He'll come back and mar-ry me,__ Bon-ny Bob-by Shaf - to!

Bob-by Shaf-to's bright and fair, pan-ning out his yel-low hair.

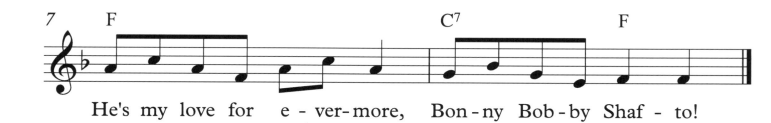

He's my love for e - ver-more, Bon-ny Bob-by Shaf - to!

F
Bobby Shafto's gone to sea,
C7
silver buckles at his knee.
F
He'll come back and marry me,
C7   **F**
Bonny Bobby Shafto!
F
Bobby Shafto's bright and fair,
C7
panning out his yellow hair.
F
He's my love for evermore,
C7   **F**
Bonny Bobby Shafto!.

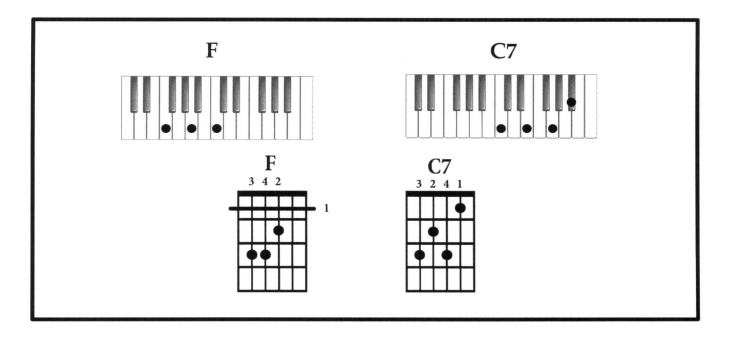

I Love Little Kitty

English nursery rhyme

I___ love lit - tle kit - ty, her coat is so warm, and_

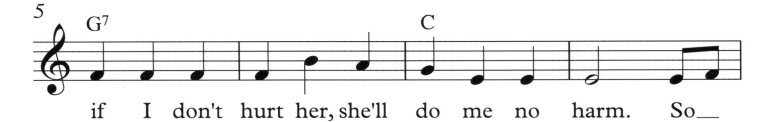

if I don't hurt her, she'll do me no harm. So__

I'll not pull her tail, nor drive her a - way, but_

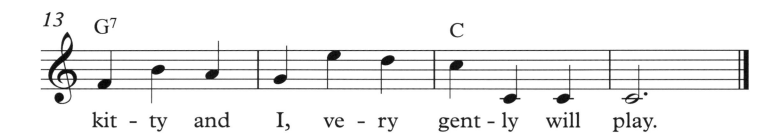

kit - ty and I, ve - ry gent - ly will play.

C

I love little kitty,

F

her coat is so warm,

G7

and if I don't hurt her,

C

she'll do me no harm.

So I'll not pull her tail,

F

nor drive her away,

G7

but kitty and I,

C

very gently will play.

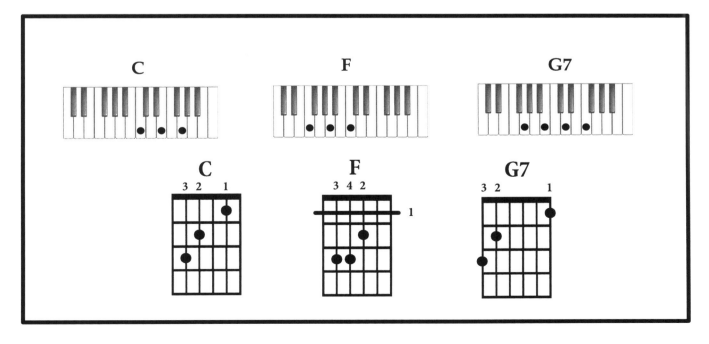

Oh Dear, What Can the Matter Be?

Nursery rhyme

Oh, dear! What can the mat-ter be? Oh, dear! What can the mat-ter be? Oh, dear! What can the mat-ter be? John ny's so long at the fair. He pro-mised he'd buy me a fair - ing should please me, and then for a kiss, oh, he vowed he would tease me. He pro-mised he'd bring me a bunch of blue rib-bons, to tie up my bon-ny brown hair.

C
Oh dear! What can the matter be?
G7
Oh, dear! What can the matter be?
C
Oh dear! what can the matter be?
  G7   C
  Johnny's so long at the fair.

  C
He promised he'd buy me a fairing should please me,
  G7
and then for a kiss, oh, he vowed he would tease me.
  C
He promised he'd bring me a bunch of blue ribbons,
   G7   C
   to tie up my bonny brown hair.

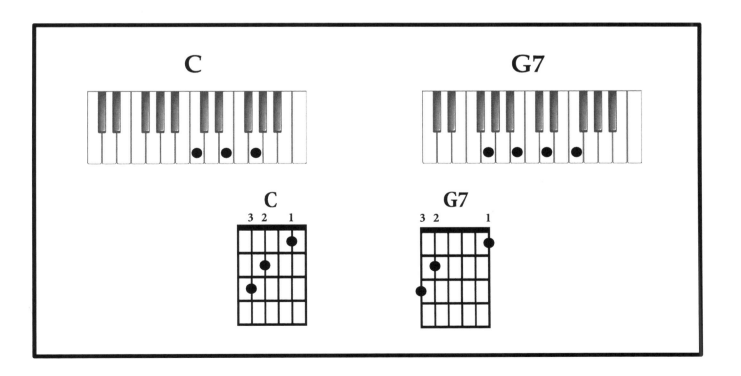

Humpty Dumpty

English nursery rhyme

Hump - ty Dump - ty sat on a wall,

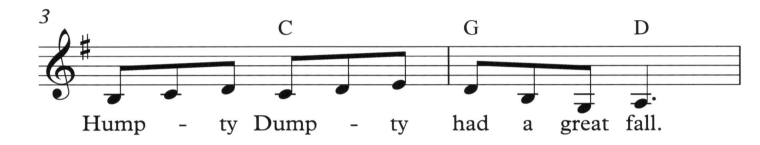

Hump - ty Dump - ty had a great fall.

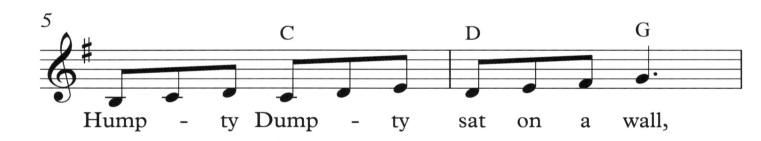

Hump - ty Dump - ty sat on a wall,

could - n't put Hump - ty to - geth - er a - gain.

   G   **C**   **D**   **G**
Humpty Dumpty sat on a wall,
      C   **G**   **D**
Humpty Dumpty had a great fall.
G   **C**   **D**   **G**
All the king's horses and all the king's men
      C   **D**   **G**
couldn't put Humpty together again.

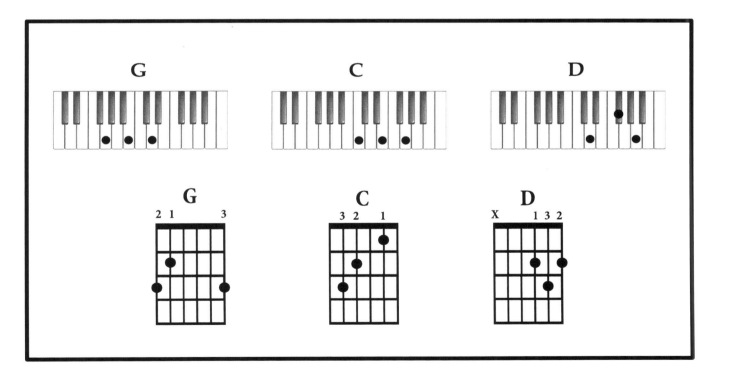

The Farmer in the Dell

Nursery rhyme

The far - mer in the dell. The far - mer in the dell.

Hi - ho, the der - ry - o. The far - mer in the dell. The

far - mer takes a wife. The far - mer takes a wife.

Hi - ho, the der - ry - o. The far - mer takes a wife.

G
The farmer in the dell.

The farmer in the dell.

Hi-ho, the derry-o.
           D   G
The farmer in the dell.

G
The farmer takes a wife.

The farmer takes a wife.

Hi-ho, the derry-o.
          D   G
The farmer takes a wife.

G
The wife takes the child.

The wife takes the child.

Hi-ho, the derry-o.
          D   G
The wife takes the child.

Continue with the following verses:

- The child takes the nurse.

- The nurse takes the cow.

- The cow takes the dog.

- The dog takes the cat.

- The cat takes the mouse(or rat).

- The mouse (or rat) takes the cheese.

- The mouse (or rat) takes the cheese.

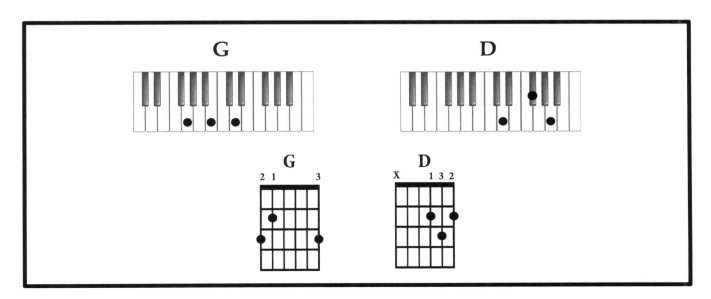

Itsy Bitsy Spider

Nursery rhyme

The it - sy bit - sy spi - der went up the wa - ter spout.

Down came the rain and washed the spi - der out.

Out came the sun and dried up all the rain. And the

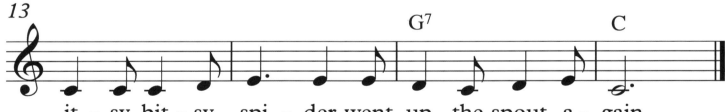

it - sy bit - sy spi - der went up the spout a - gain.

C
The itsy bitsy spider
G7   C
went up the waterspout.

Down came the rain
G7   C
and washed the spider out.

Out came the sun
G7   C
and dried up all the rain.

And the itsy bitsy spider
G7   C
went up the spout again.

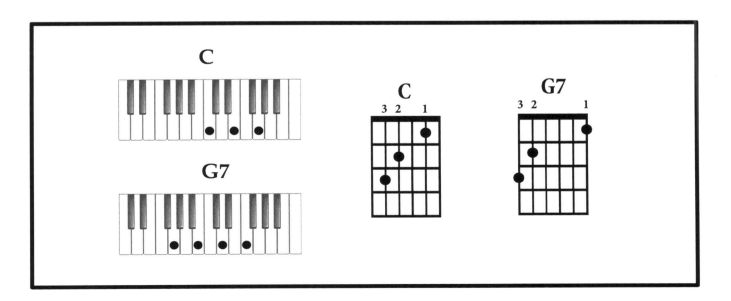

Row, Row, Row Your Boat

English nursery rhyme

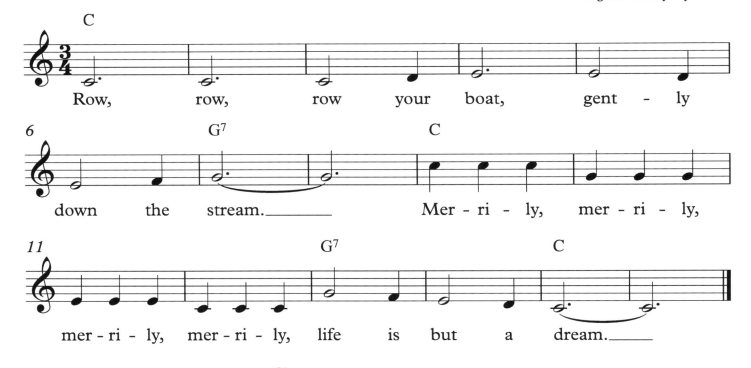

C
Row, row, row your boat,
  G7
gently down the stream.
  C
Merrily, merrily, merrily, merrily,
  G7   C
life is but a dream.

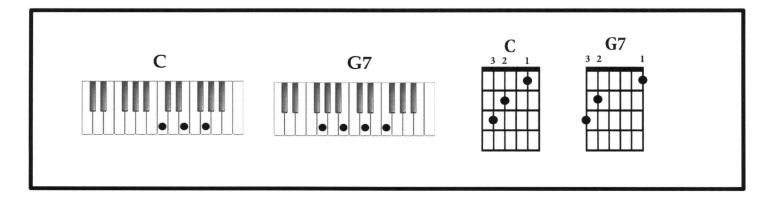

Mary, Mary, Quite Contrary

English nursery rhyme

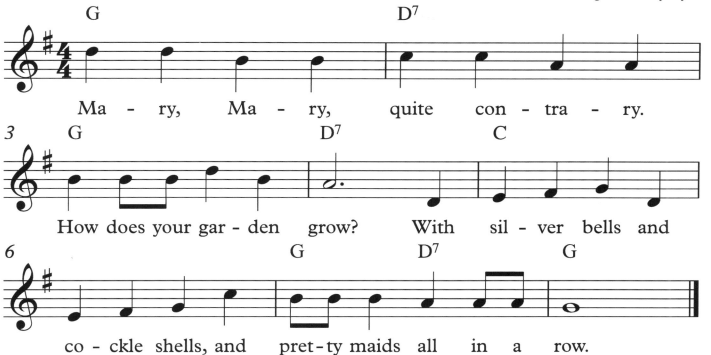

G   D7
Mary, Mary, quite contrary.
G   D7
How does your garden grow?
C
With silver bells and cockle shells,
G   D7   G
and pretty maids all in a row.

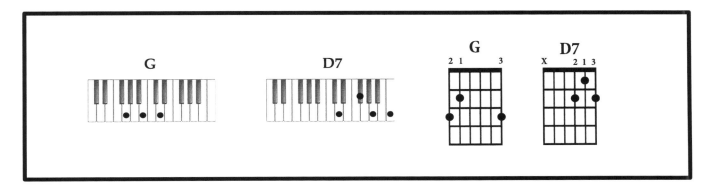

One, Two, Three, Four, Five

English nursery rhyme

One, two, three, four, five, once I caught a fish a - live.

Six, se - ven, eight, nine, ten, then I let it go a - gain.

Why did you let it go? Be - cause it bit my fin - ger so.

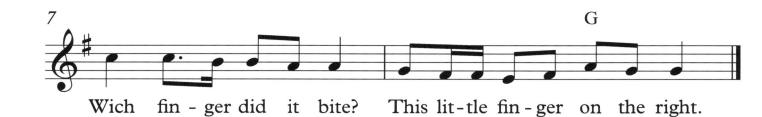

Wich fin - ger did it bite? This lit - tle fin - ger on the right.

G
One, two, three, four, five,
       D7
once I caught a fish alive.

Six, seven, eight, nine, ten,
       G
then I let it go again.

G
Why did you let it go?
       D7
Because it bit my finger so.

Which finger did it bite?
       G
This little finger on the right.

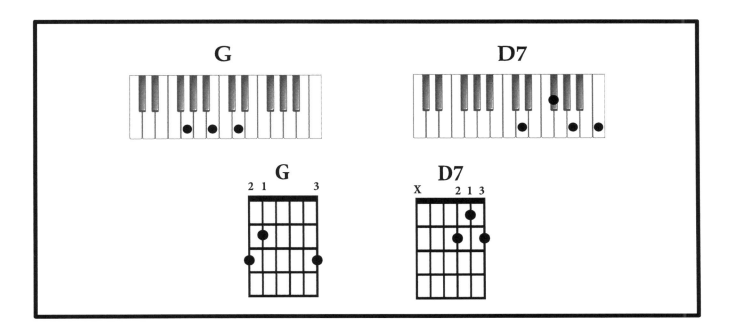

Jack Sprat

Nursery rhyme

Jack Sprat could eat no fat. His wife could eat no lean. And

so be tween them both, you see. They licked the plat ter clean.

C
Jack Sprat could eat no fat.
G
His wife could eat no lean.
F   Em   Am
And so between them both, you see
G   C
They licked the platter clean.

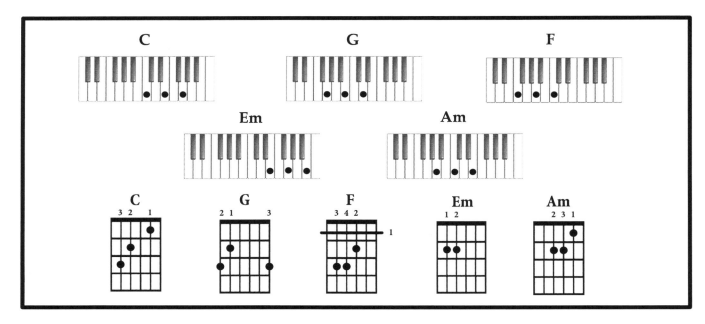

duviPlay

Tom, Tom, the Piper's Son

English nursery rhyme

Tom, Tom, the pi - per's son, stole a___ pig, and a -
way did run. The pig was eat and Tom was beat, and
Tom went___ cry - ing down the street.

C
Tom, Tom, the piper's son,
G7
stole a pig, and away did run.

The pig was eat and Tom was beat,
C
and Tom went crying down the street.

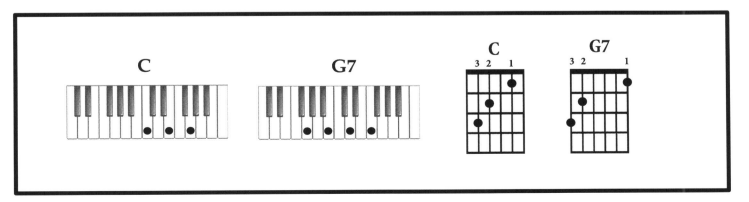

This Old Man

English nursery rhyme

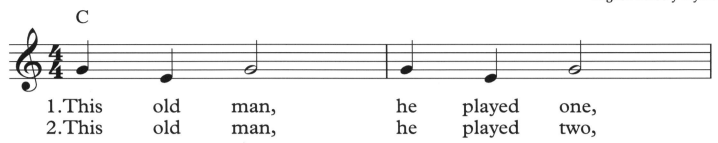

1. This old man, he played one,
2. This old man, he played two,

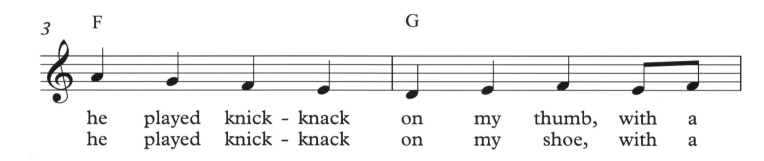

he played knick - knack on my thumb, with a
he played knick - knack on my shoe, with a

knick - knack pad - dy - whack, give the dog a bone,
knick - knack pad - dy - whack, give the dog a bone,

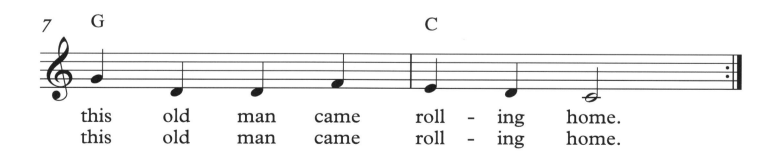

this old man came roll - ing home.
this old man came roll - ing home.

C
1. This old man, he played one,
F   G
he played knick-knack on my thumb,
           C
with a knick-knack paddywhack,

     give the dog a bone,
   G   C
this old man came rolling home.

(all verses follow the same chord progression)

2. This old man, he played two,
he played knick-knack on my shoe,
with a knick-knack paddywhack,
give the dog a bone,
this old man came rolling home.

3. This old man, he played three,
he played knick-knack on my knee,
with a knick-knack paddywhack,
give the dog a bone,
this old man came rolling home.

4. This old man, he played four,
he played knick-knack on my door,
with a knick-knack paddywhack,
give the dog a bone,
this old man came rolling home.

5. This old man, he played five,
he played knick-knack on my hive,
with a knick-knack paddywhack,
give the dog a bone,
this old man came rolling home.

6. This old man, he played six,
he played knick-knack on my sticks,
with a knick-knack paddywhack,
give the dog a bone,
this old man came rolling home.

7. This old man, he played seven,
he played knick-knack up in heaven,
with a knick-knack paddywhack,
give the dog a bone,
this old man came rolling home.

8. This old man, he played eight,
he played knick-knack on my gate,
with a knick-knack paddywhack,
give the dog a bone,
this old man came rolling home.

9. This old man, he played nine,
he played knick-knack on my spine,
with a knick-knack paddywhack,
give the dog a bone,
this old man came rolling home.

10. This old man, he played ten,
he played knick-knack once again,
with a knick-knack paddywhack,
give the dog a bone,
this old man came rolling home.

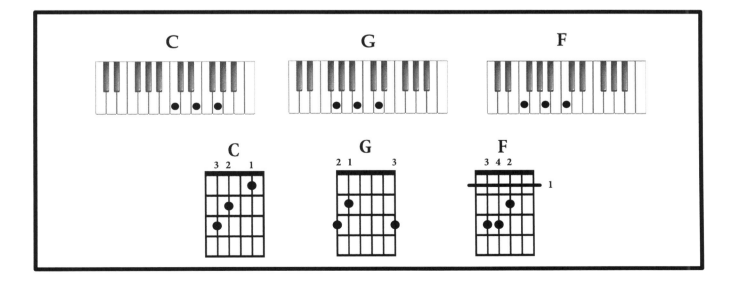

Ride a Cock-Horse to Banbury Cross

English nursery rhyme

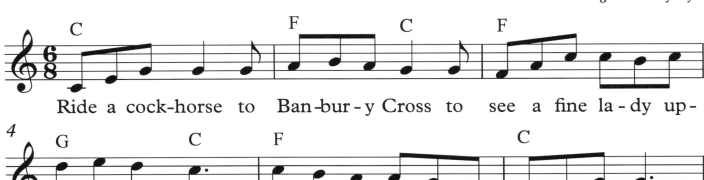

Ride a cock-horse to Ban-bur-y Cross to see a fine la-dy up-

on a white horse, rings on her fin-gers and bells on her toes.

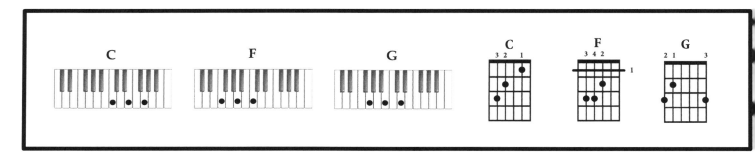

She shall have mu-sic wher-e-ver she goes.

         C   F   C
Ride a cock-horse to Banbury Cross
         F   G   C
to see a fine lady upon a white horse,
  F   C
rings on her fingers and bells on her toes.
 G   C
She shall have music wherever she goes.

Pease Porridge Hot

Nursery rhyme

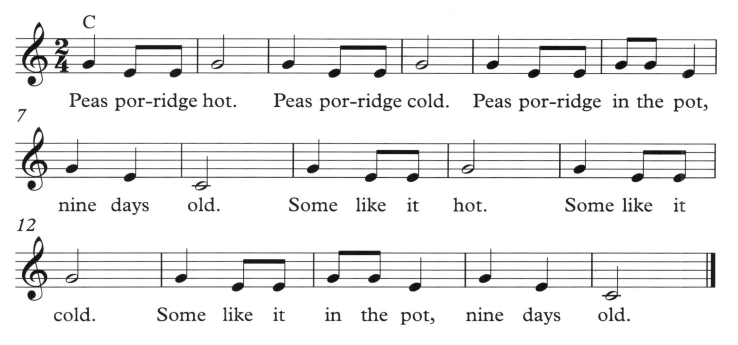

Peas por-ridge hot. Peas por-ridge cold. Peas por-ridge in the pot,

nine days old. Some like it hot. Some like it

cold. Some like it in the pot, nine days old.

C
1. Pease porridge hot.
Pease porridge cold.
Pease porridge in the pot,
nine days old.

C
2. Some like it hot.
Some like it cold.
Some like it in the pot,
nine days old.

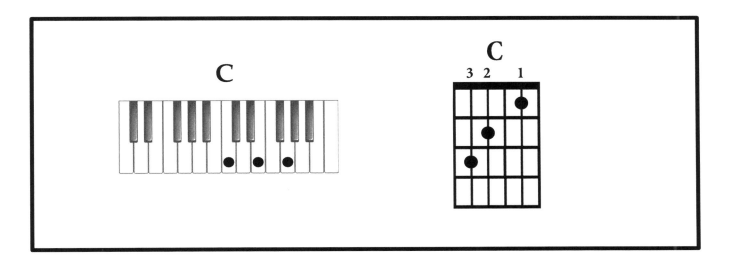

A-Tisket, A-Tasket

Nursery rhyme

A - tis - ket, a - tas - ket, a   green and yel-low bask - ket. I

wrote a let - ter   to my love and   on the way I   dropped it, I

dropped it, I   dropped it, and   on the way I   dropped it. A

lit - tle boy he   picked it up and   put it   in his   poc - ket.

C
A-tisket, a-tasket,

a green and yellow basket.
G7
I wrote a letter to my love
C
and on the way I dropped it,

I dropped it, I dropped it,

and on the way I dropped it.
G7   **C**
A little boy he picked it up and put it in his pocket.

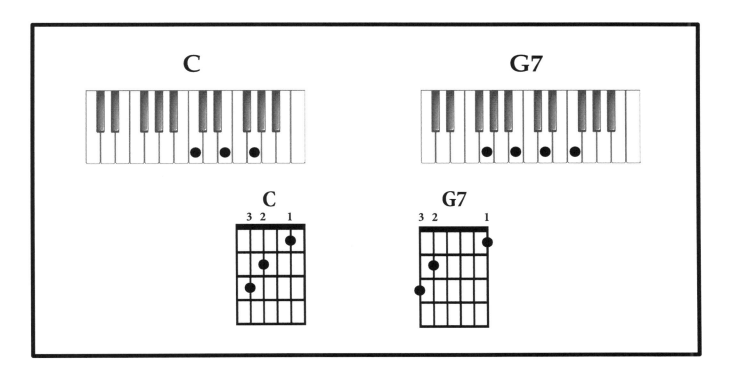

Hot Cross Buns

English nursery rhyme

Hot   cross   buns.   Hot   cross   buns.

One a pen - ny, two a pen - ny, hot cross buns.

C   G7   C
Hot cross buns.
G7   C
Hot cross buns.
G7
One a penny, two a penny,
C   G7   C
hot cross buns.

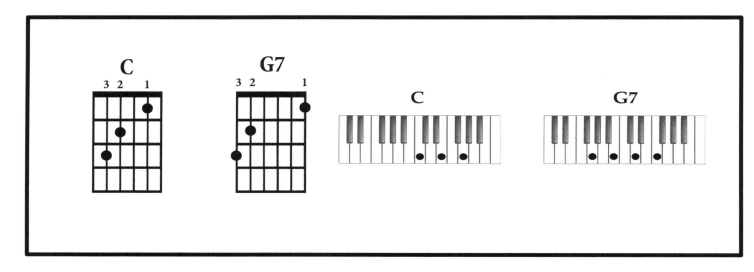

Diddle, Diddle, Dumpling, My Son John

English nursery rhyme

Did-dle, did-dle, dump-ling, my son John. Went to bed with his

trou-sers on. One shoe off and one shoe on.

Did-dle, did-dle, dump-ling, my son John.

    F   **Bb** **F**
Diddle, diddle, dumpling, my son John.
   C7   **F**
Went to bed with his trousers on.
        Bb **F**
One shoe off and one shoe on.
   C7   **F**
Diddle, diddle, dumpling, my son John.

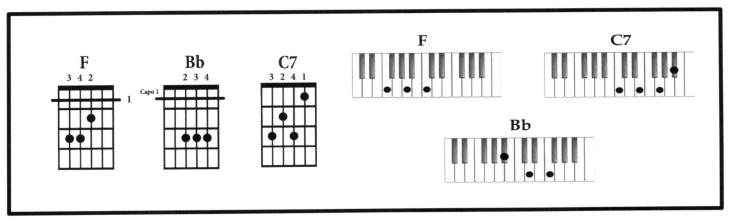

Little Robin Redbreast

Nursery rhyme

1.Lit - tle Ro - bin Red - breast sat up - on a tree.
2.Lit - tle Ro - bin Red - breast jumped up - on a spade.

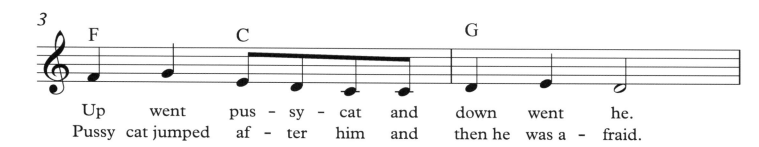

Up went pus - sy - cat and down went he.
Pussy cat jumped af - ter him and then he was a - fraid.

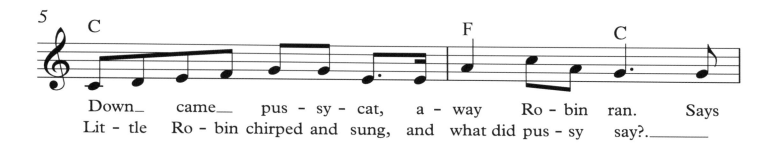

Down_ came_ pus - sy - cat, a - way Ro - bin ran. Says
Lit - tle Ro - bin chirped and sung, and what did pus - sy say?._____

lit - tle Ro - bin Red___ breast: "Catch me if you can".
Pus - sy - cat said: "Mew, mew, mew" and Ro - bin flew a - way.

C
1. Little Robin Redbreast
   F   C
   sat upon a tree,
  F   C
  Up went pussycat
      G
  and down went he.
C
  Down came pussycat,
     F   C
   away Robin ran.
 F   C
Says little Robin Redbreast:
 G   C
 "Catch me if you can".

C
2. Little Robin Redbreast
   F   C
   jumped upon a spade.
 F   C
 Pussycat jumped after him
      G
 and then he was afraid.
C
 Little Robin chirped and sung,
      F   C
 and what did pussy say?
F   C
Pussycat said: "Mew, mew, mew"
      G   C
 and Robin flew away.

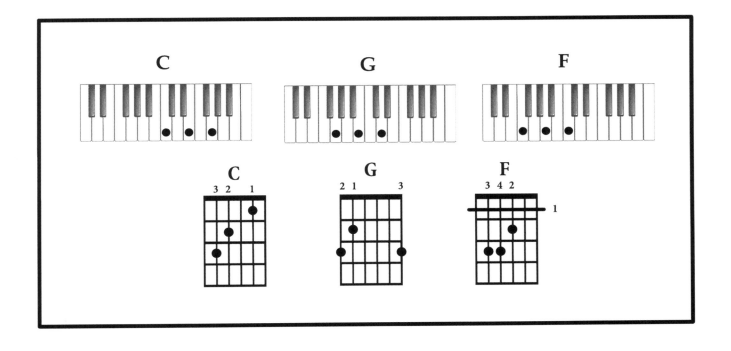

Ring a Ring o' Roses

Nursery rhyme

Ring - a - ring - o'   ro - ses,   a   pock - et   full   of

po - sies, a - ti - shoo, a   ti - shoo, we   all   fall   down.

C
Ring-a-ring o' roses,

A pocket full of posies,

A-tishoo, a-tishoo,
G   C
We all fall down.

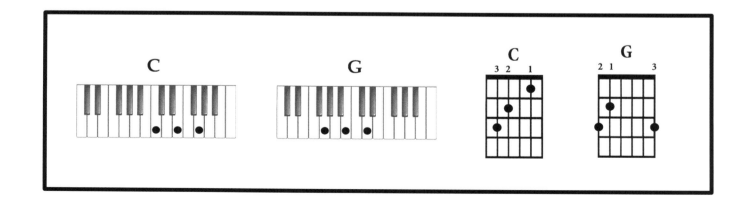

Little Tommy Tucker

English nursery rhyme

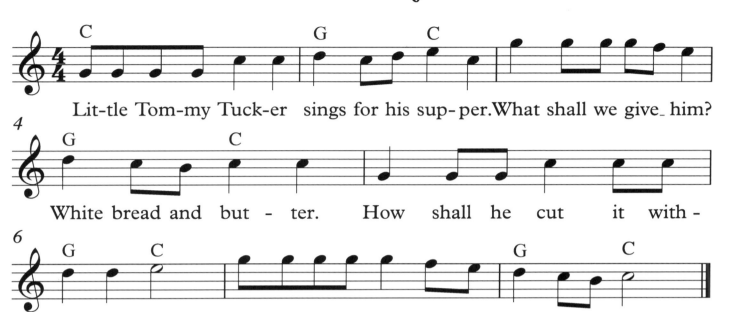

Lit-tle Tom-my Tuck-er sings for his sup-per. What shall we give_ him?

White bread and but - ter.   How   shall he   cut   it   with -

out   a knife?   How will he be mar-ried with-out   a___ wife.

C
Little Tom Tucker
G   C
sings for his supper.

What shall we give him?
G   C
White bread and butter.

How shall he cut it
G   C
Without a knife?

How will he be married
G   C
Without a wife?

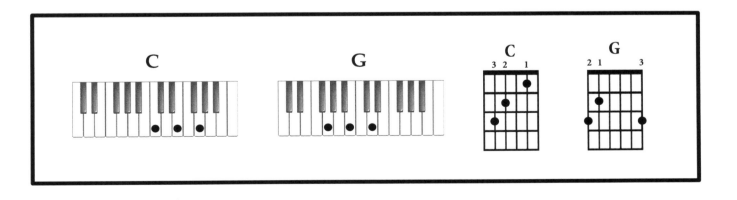

Lucy Locket

Nursery rhyme

Lu - cy Lock-et   lost her po-cket, Kit - ty Fish-er   found - it.

Not a pen-ny   was there in   it,   on - ly rib-bons 'round it.

C   F   C
Lucy Locket lost her pocket,
F   C
Kitty Fisher found it.
F   C
Not a penny was there in it,
F   C
only ribbons 'round it.

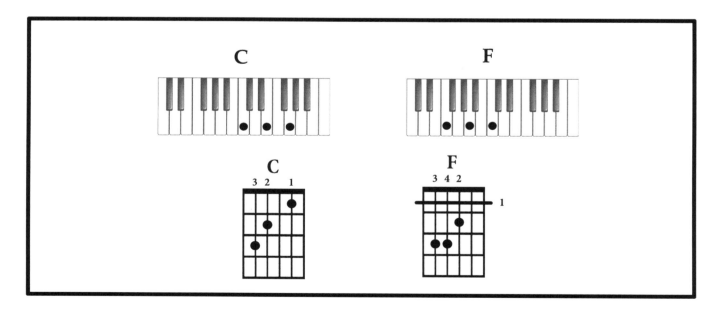

See-saw Margery Daw

Nursery rhyme

See - saw, Mer-ge-ry Daw, Jack shall have a new

mas - ter. He shall have but a pen-ny a day. Be -

cause he won't work a - ny fas - ter.

C
See-saw, Margery Day,
Jack shall have a new master.
He shall have but a penny a day.
Because he won't work any faster.

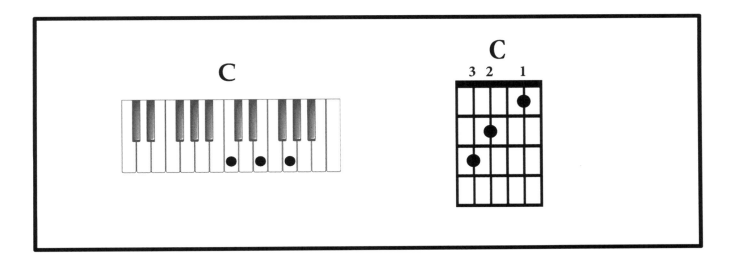

The Grand Old Duke of York

English children's nursery rhyme

Oh, the grand old Duke of York, he had ten thou sand men. He

marched them up to the top of the hill and he marched them down a - gain. And

when they were up, they were up, and when they were down, they were down. And

when they were on - ly half - way up they were nei - ther up nor down.

C
Oh, the grand old Duke of York,
G
he had ten thousand men.
C   F
He marched them up to the top of the hill,
C   G   C
and he marched them down again.

C
And when they were up, they were up.
G
And when they were down, they were down.
C   F
And when they were only half-way up,
C   G   C
they were neither up nor down.

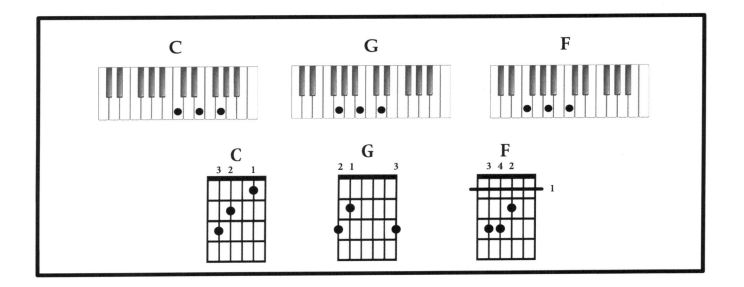

The Great Songbook of Nursery Rhymes

Little Boy Blue

Nursery rhyme

Lit - tle boy blue, come blow___ your horn. The

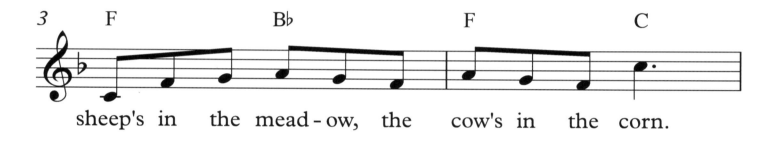

sheep's in the mead - ow, the cow's in the corn.

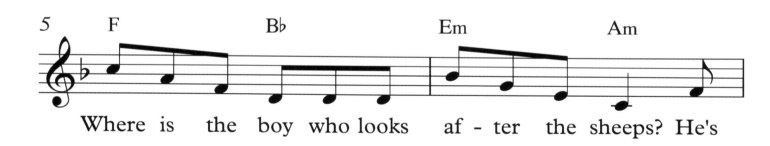

Where is the boy who looks af - ter the sheeps? He's

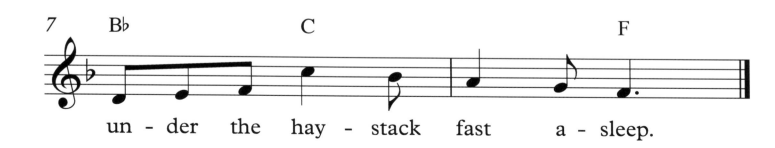

un - der the hay - stack fast a - sleep.

F   C
Little boy blue,
  F   C
come blow your horn.
 F   Bb
The sheep's in the meadow,
  F   C
the cow's in the corn.
 F   Bb
Where is the boy
   Em   Am
who looks after the sheeps?
 Bb   C
He's under the haystack
    F
fast asleep.

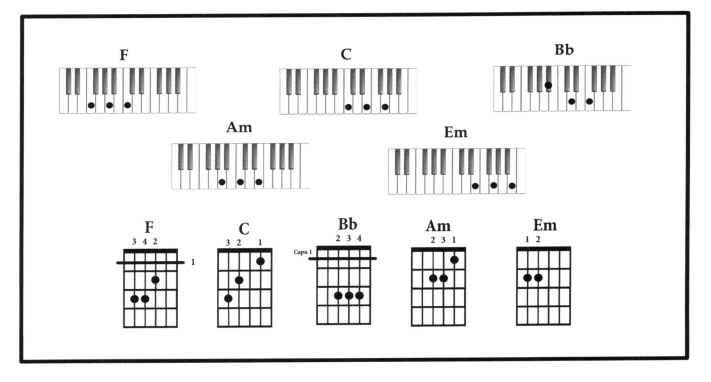

Girls and Boys Come Out to Play

Nursery rhyme

Girls and boys come out to play, The moon doth shine as bright as day.

Leave your sup‑per and leave your sleep, and come to your play‑fel‑lows

down the street. Come with a whoop, come with a call,___

come with good will___ or not at all. Up the lad‑der and

down the wall, a half‑pen‑ny roll___ will serve us all.

C   G7   C

Girls and boys come out to play,

  G7   C

The moon doth shine as bright as day.

          G7   C

Leave your supper and leave your sleep,

 G7   C

and come with your playfellows down the street.

                    F

Come with a whoop, come with a call,

  C

come with a good will or not at all.

                   F

Up the ladder and down the wall,

   C

a halfpenny roll will serve us all.

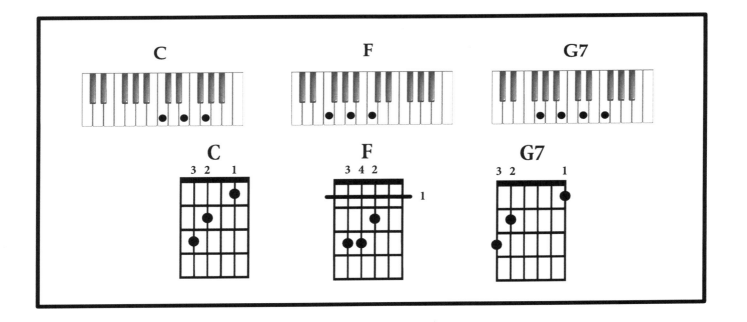

Mary Had a Little Lamb

Nursery rhyme

1.Ma – ry had a lit – tle lamb, lit – tle lamb, lit – tle lamb.
fol – lowed her to school one day, school one day, school one day. He

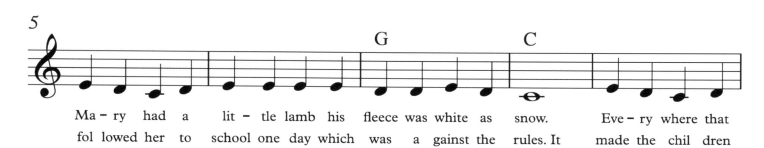

Ma – ry had a lit – tle lamb his fleece was white as snow. Eve – ry where that
fol lowed her to school one day which was a gainst the rules. It made the chil dren

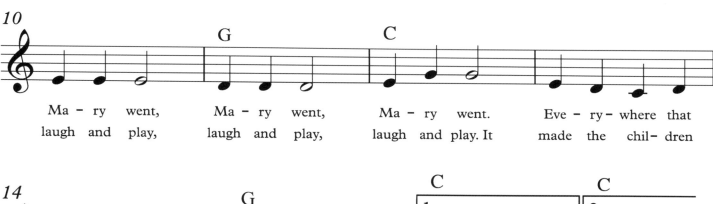

Ma – ry went, Ma – ry went, Ma – ry went. Eve – ry – where that
laugh and play, laugh and play, laugh and play. It made the chil – dren

Ma – ry went the lamb was sure to go. 2.He
laugh and play to see a lamb in school.

duviPlay

C
Mary had a little lamb,
G   C
little lamb, little lamb.

Mary had a little lamb
G   C
his fleece was white as snow.

C
Everywhere that Mary went,
G   C
Mary went, Mary went.

Everywhere that Mary went
G   C
the lamb was sure to go.

C
He followed her to school one day,
G   C
school one day, school one day.

He followed her to school one day
G   C
which was against the rules.

C
It made the children laugh and play,
G   C
laugh and play, laugh and play.

It made the children laugh and play
G   C
to see a lamb at school.

C
And so the teacher turned it out,
G   C
turned it out, turned it out.

And so the teacher turned it out
G   C
but still it lingered near.

C
And waited patiently about,
G   C
patiently about, patiently about.

And waited patiently about
G   C
till Mary did appear.

C
Why does the lamb love Mary so?
G   C
Mary so?, Mary so?.

Why does the lamb love Mary so?
G   C
The eager children cry.

C
Why, Mary loves the lamb, you know,
G   C
lamb you know, lamb you know.

Why, Mary loves the lamb, you know.
G   C
The teacher did reply.

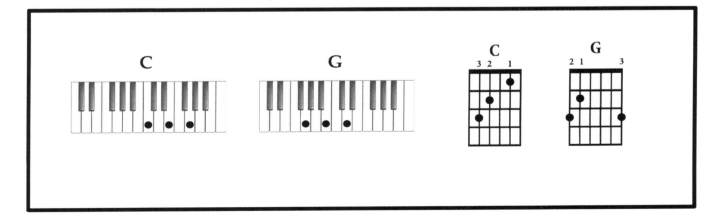

Scotland's Burning

Nursery rhyme

Scot-land's burn-ing, Scot-land's burn-ing. Look out, look out,

fire! fire! fire! fire! Pour on wa__ ter, Pour on wa__ ter.

F
Scotland's burning, Scotland's Burning.
     C   F   C   F
    Look out, look out
    C
    Fire! fire! fire! fire!
F
Pour on water, pour on water.

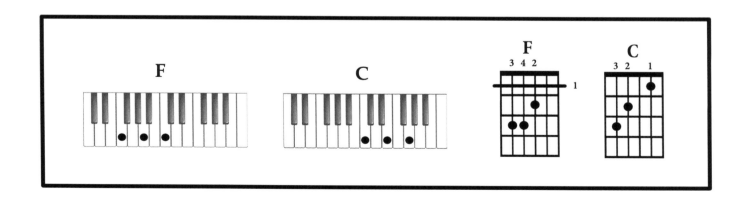

Jack and Jill

Nursery rhyme

Jack and Jill went up the hill to fetch a pail of wa - ter.

Jack fell down and broke his crown and Jill came tumb-ling af - ter.

    C   **F**
1. Jack and Jill
    C   **F**
Went up the hill
  C   **F** **C**
To fetch a pail of water,
     F
Jack fell down
     C
And broke his crown
G7   **C**
And Jill came tumbling after.

    C   **F**
2. Up Jack got
    C   **F**
And home did trot
  C   **F** **C**
As fast as he could caper,
     F
Went to bed
     C
To mend his head
G7   **C**
With vinegar and brown paper.

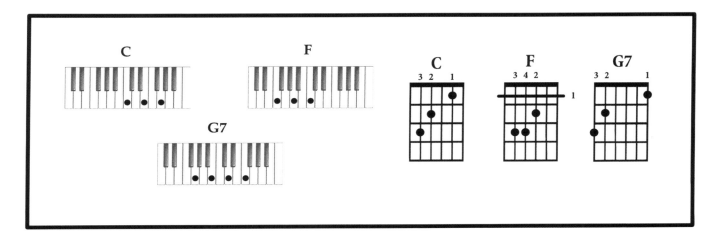

Baa, Baa, Black Sheep

English nursery rhyme

Baa, baa, black sheep, have you a - ny wool? yes sir, yes sir,

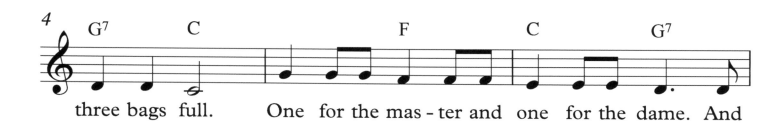

three bags full.   One for the mas - ter and one for the dame. And

one   for   the   lit - tle   boy   who   lives   down   the   lane.

C
Baa, baa, black sheep,
  F   C
Have you any wool?
  G7   C
  Yes sir, yes sir,
  G7   C
  three bags full.
              F
One for the master
    C   G7
and one for the dame.
    C   F
And one for the little boy
    C   G7   C
who lives down the lane.

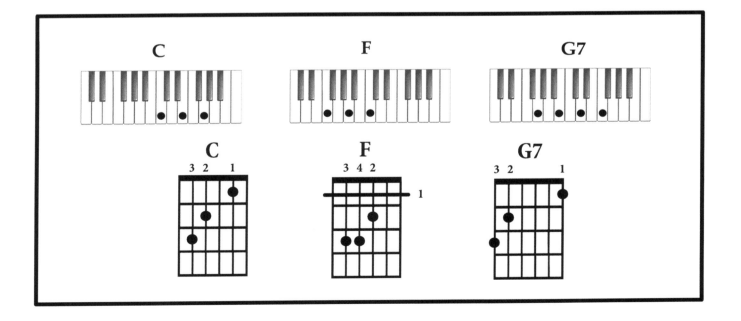

London Bridge is Falling Down

English nursery rhyme

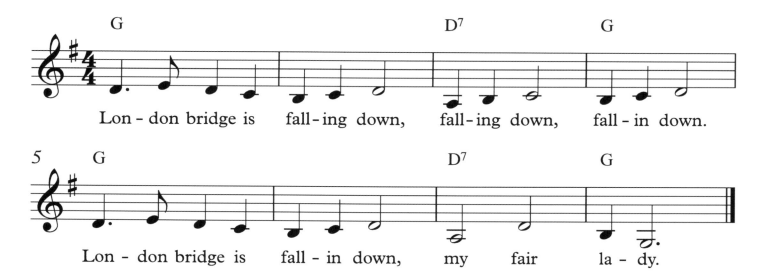

Lon - don bridge is fall-ing down, fall-ing down, fall-in down.

Lon - don bridge is fall - in down, my fair la - dy.

G
London bridge is falling down,
   D7   **G**
  falling down, falling down.
G
London bridge is falling down,
     D7   **G**
   my fair lady.

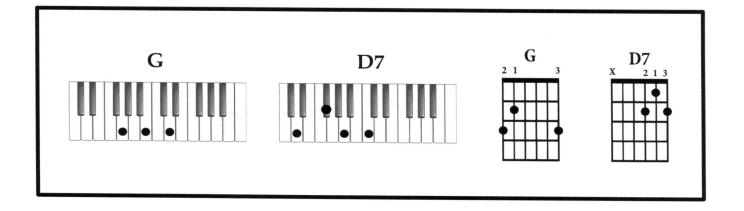

Hey Diddle Diddle

English nursery rhyme

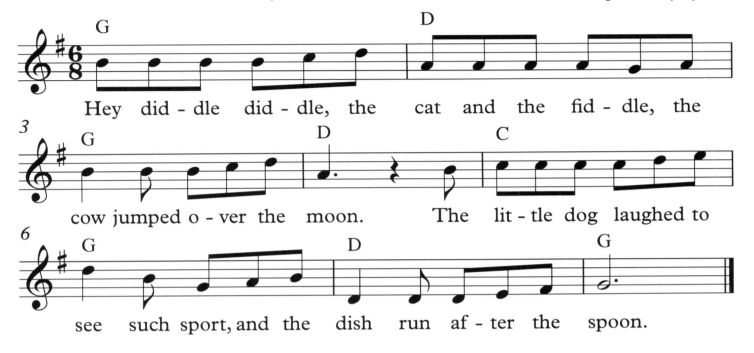

Hey did - dle did - dle, the cat and the fid - dle, the

cow jumped o - ver the moon. The lit - tle dog laughed to

see such sport, and the dish run af - ter the spoon.

G
Hey diddle diddle,
D
the cat and the fiddle,
G   **D**
the cow jumped over the moon.
C
The little dog laughed
G
to see such sport,
D   **G**
and the dish ran after the spoon.

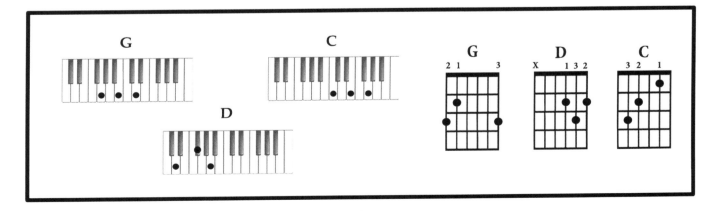

There Was a Crooked Man

English nursery rhyme

There was a crook-ed man, who walked a crook-ed mile. He

found a crook-ed six - pence up - on a crook-ed stile. He

bought a crook-ed cat which caught a crook-ed mouse, and they

all lived to - ge - ther in a lit - tle crook-ed house.

C
There was a crooked man,
G
who walked a crooked mile.
C
He found a crooked sixpence
G
upon a crooked stile.
C
He bought a crooked cat,
G
which caught a crooked mouse,
C   G
and they all lived together
C
in a little crooked house.

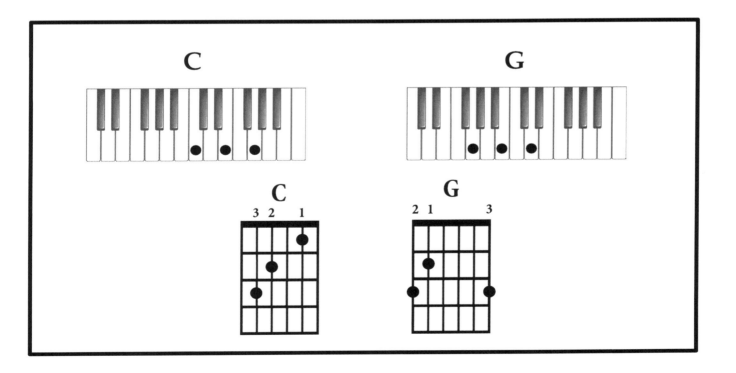

Sing a Song of Sixpence

English nursery rhyme

Sing a song of six - pence, a poc - ket full of rye.

Four and twen - ty black - birds, baked in a pie.

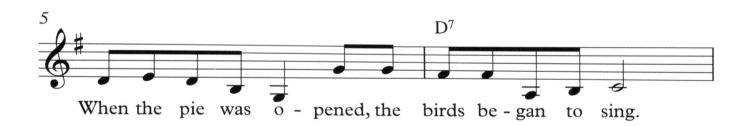

When the pie was o - pened, the birds be - gan to sing.

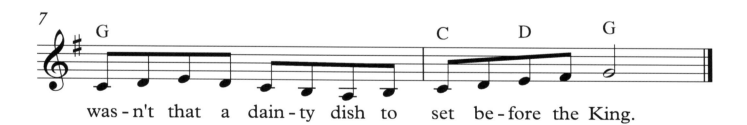

was - n't that a dain - ty dish to set be - fore the King.

G
Sing a song of sixpence,
   D7
   a pocket full of rye.

Four and twenty blackbirds,
   G
   baked in a pie.

When the pie was opened,
   D7
   the birds began to sing.
G
Wasn't that a dainty dish
   C   D   G
   to set before the King.

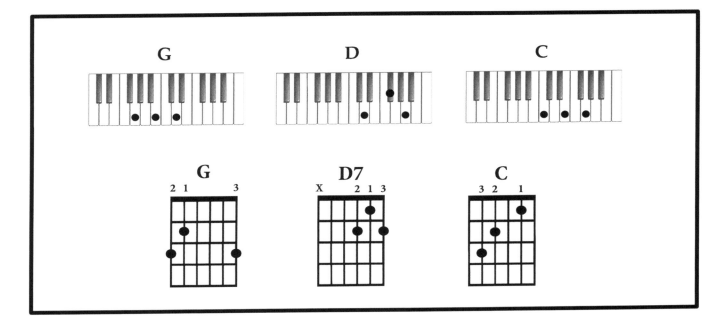

Hickory Dickory Dock

English nursery rhyme

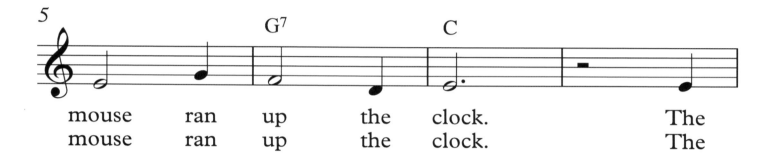

1.Hick - o - ry, dick - o - ry, dock. The
2.Hick - o - ry, dick - o - ry, dick. The

mouse ran up the clock. The
mouse ran up the clock. The

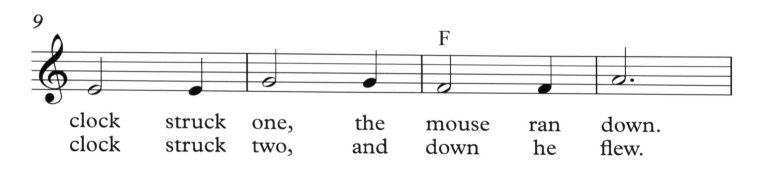

clock struck one, the mouse ran down.
clock struck two, and down he flew.

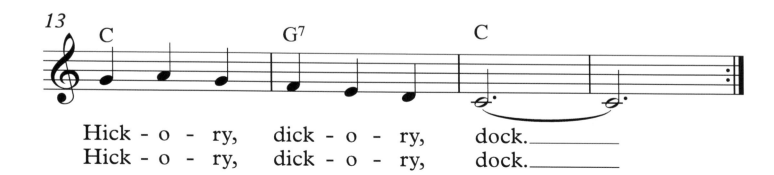

Hick - o - ry, dick - o - ry, dock._____
Hick - o - ry, dick - o - ry, dock._____

```
    C        G7        C
    1. Hickory, dickory, dock.
             G7        C
    The mouse ran up the clock.

       The clock struck one,
    F
       the mouse ran down.
    C        G7        C
       Hickory, dickory, dock.
```

All verses follow the same chord progression.

2. Hickory, dickory, dock.
The mouse ran up the clock,
The clock struck two
And down he flew,
Hickory, dickory, dock.

3. Hickory, dickory, dock.
The mouse ran up the clock,
The clock struck three
And he did flee,
Hickory, dickory, dock.

4. Hickory, dickory, dock.
The mouse ran up the clock,
The clock struck four,
He hit the floor,
Hickory, dickory, dock.

5. Hickory, dickory, dock.
The mouse ran up the clock,
The clock struck five,
The mouse took a dive,
Hickory, dickory, dock.

6. Hickory, dickory, dock.
The mouse ran up the clock,
The clock struck six,
That mouse, he split,
Hickory, dickory, dock.

7. Hickory, dickory, dock.
The mouse ran up the clock,
The clock struck seven,
8, 9, 10, 11,
Hickory, dickory, dock.

8. Hickory, dickory, dock.
The mouse ran up the clock,
As twelve bells rang,
The mousie sprang,
Hickory, dickory, dock.

9. Hickory, dickory, dock.
"Why scamper?" asked the clock,
"You scare me so
I have to go!
Hickory, dickory, dock."

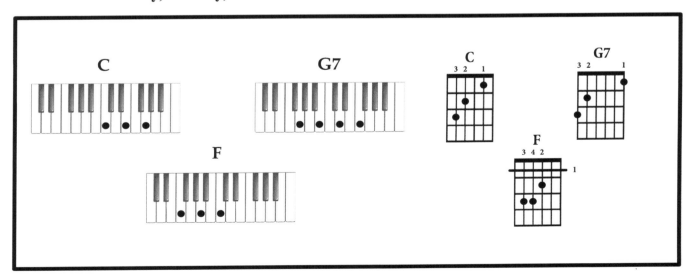

Pop! Goes the Weasel

English nursery rhyme

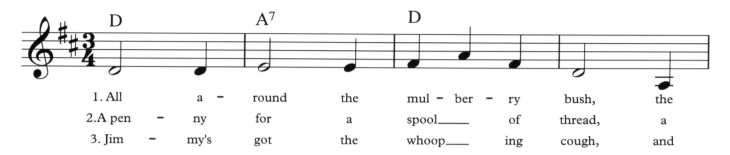

1. All a - round the mul - ber - ry bush, the
2. A pen - ny for a spool____ of thread, a
3. Jim - my's got the whoop____ ing cough, and

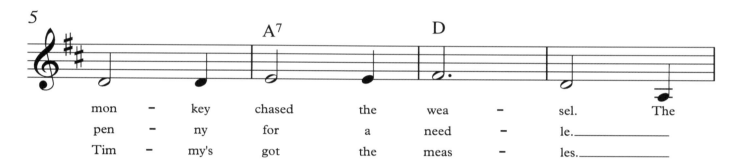

mon - key chased the wea - sel. The
pen - ny for a need - le._____
Tim - my's got the meas - les._____

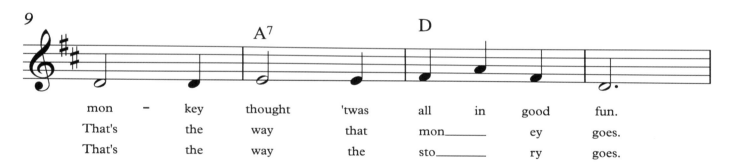

mon - key thought 'twas all in good fun.
That's the way that mon____ ey goes.
That's the way the sto____ ry goes.

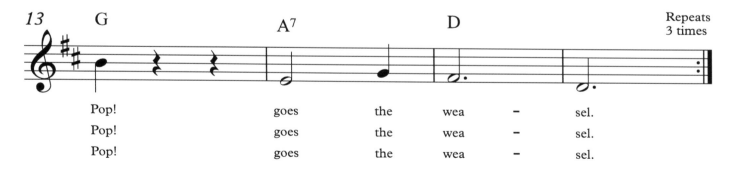

Repeats 3 times

Pop! goes the wea - sel.
Pop! goes the wea - sel.
Pop! goes the wea - sel.

D   A7   D
All around the mulberry bush,
              A7   D
the monkey chased the weasel.
        A7   D
The monkey thought 'twas all in good fun,
        G   A7   D
Pop! goes the weasel.

    D   A7   D
A penny for a spool of thread,
            A7   D
a penny for a needle
        A7   D
That's the way the money goes,
      G   A7   D
Pop! goes the weasel.

D   A7   D
Jimmy's got the whooping cough
              A7   D
and Timmy's got the measles.
        A7   D
That's the way the story goes,
      G   A7   D
Pop! goes the weasel.

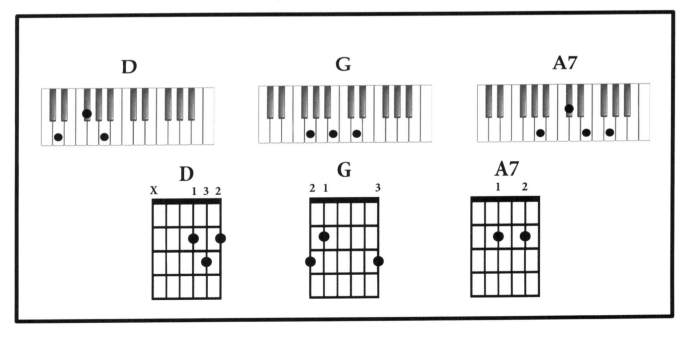

Oranges and Lemons

English nursery rhyme

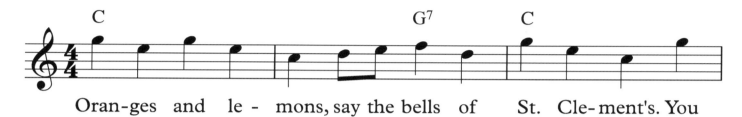

Oran-ges and le - mons, say the bells of St. Cle-ment's. You

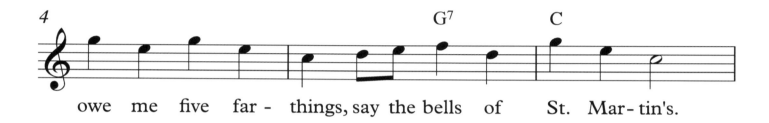

owe me five far - things, say the bells of St. Mar-tin's.

When will you pay me? Say the bells of old Bai - ley.

When I grow rich, say the bells of Shore ditch.

duviPlay

When will that be?___ Say the bells of Step- ney.___

I do not know,___ say the great bell of Bow.___

Here comes a can - dle to___ light you to bed, and

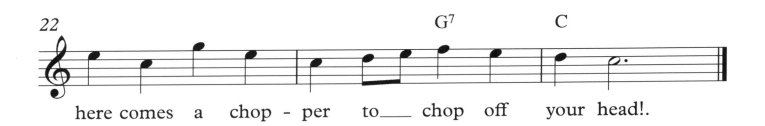

here comes a chop - per to___ chop off your head!.

C
Oranges and lemons,
   G7   C
say the bells of St. Clement's.

You owe me five farthings,
   G7   C
say the bells of St. Martin's.
 G
When will you pay me?
 D7   G
Say the bells of Old Bailey.

When I grow rich,
 D7   G
say the bells of Shoreditch.
 C
When will that be?
  G7   C
say the bells of Stepney.

I do not know,
 G7   C
says the great bell of Bow.

Here comes a candle
 G7   C
to light you to bed,

and here comes a chopper
 G7   C
to chop off your head!

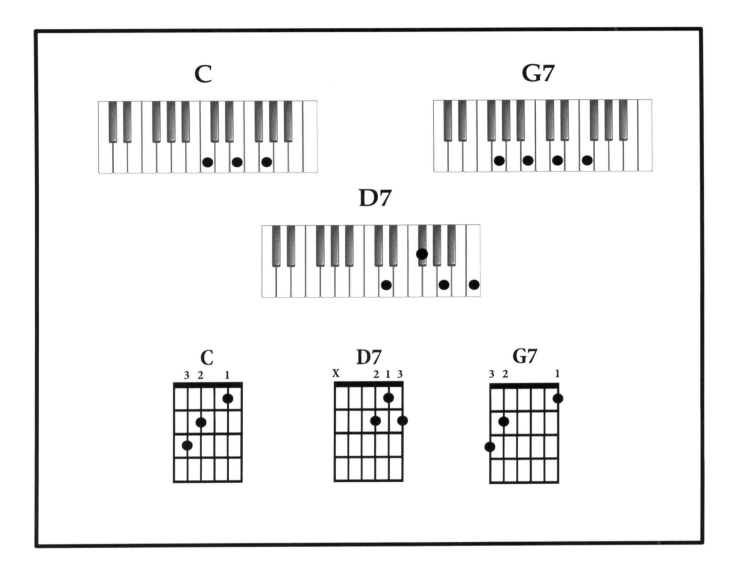

Bye, Baby Bunting

English nursery rhyme

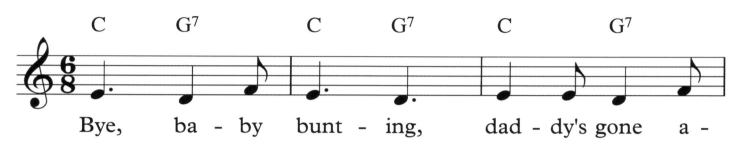

Bye, ba - by bunt - ing, dad - dy's gone a -

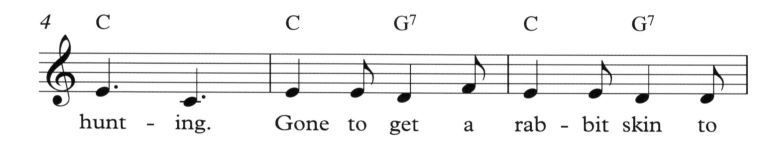

hunt - ing. Gone to get a rab - bit skin to

wrap the ba - by Bun - ting in.

duviPlay

    C   G7   C   G7
Bye, baby Bunting,
C   G7   C
daddy's gone a-hunting.
C   G7   C   G7
Gone to get a rabbit skin
C   G7   C
to wrap the baby Bunting in.

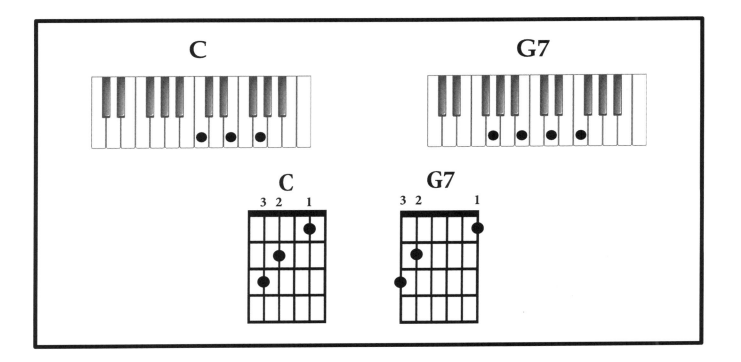

Basic piano chords

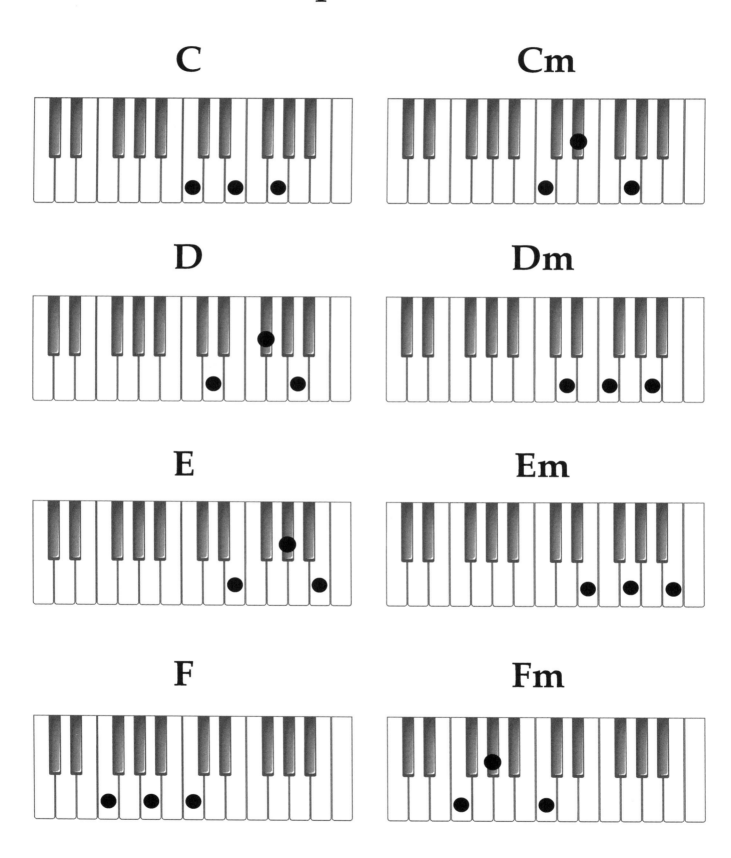

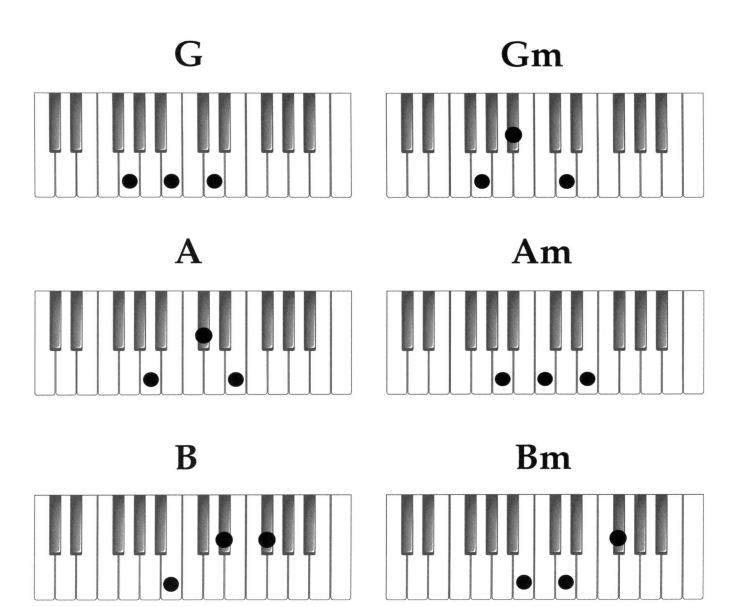

Basic 7th chords

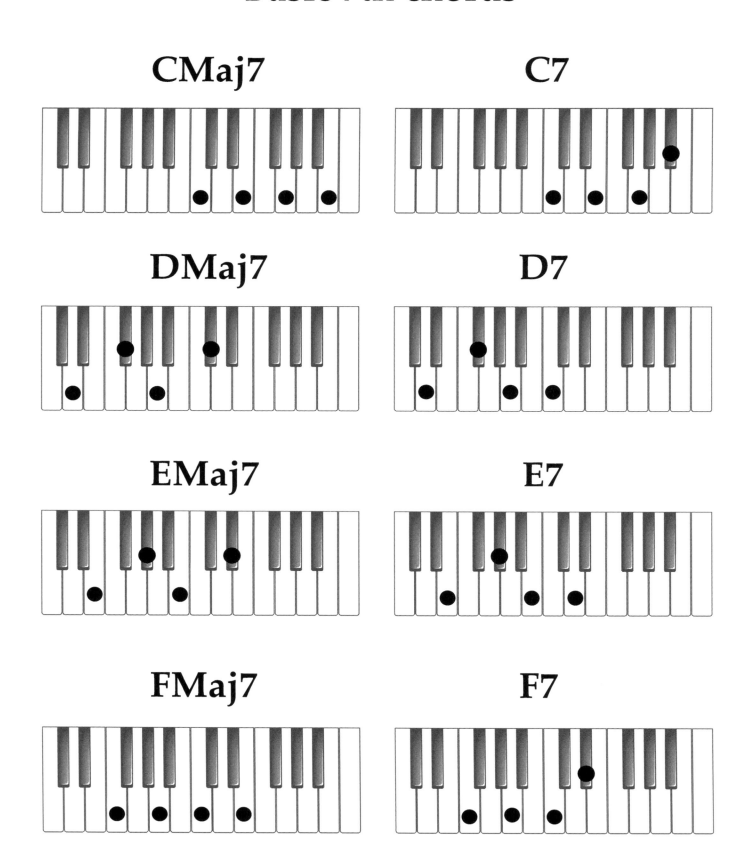

CMaj7

C7

DMaj7

D7

EMaj7

E7

FMaj7

F7

GMaj7

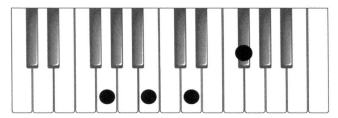

G7

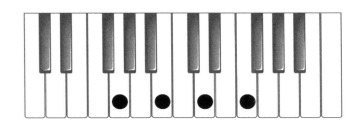

AMaj7

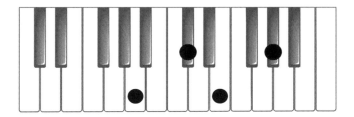

A7

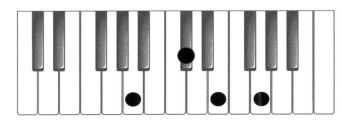

BMaj7

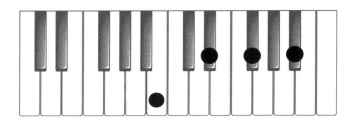

B7

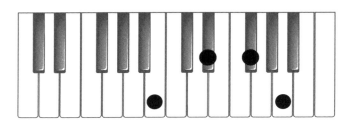

Basic guitar chords

C
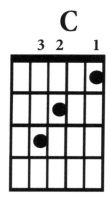

Cm

D
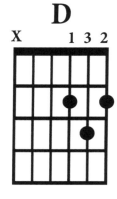

Dm
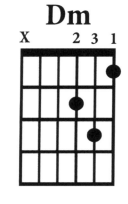

E
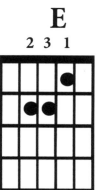

Em
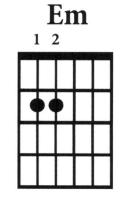

F
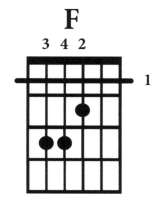

Fm
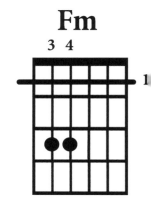

G
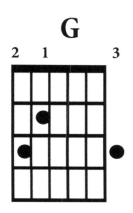

Gm
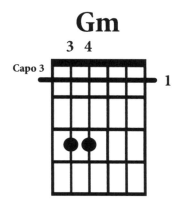

A
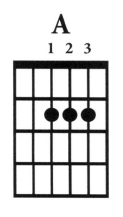

Am
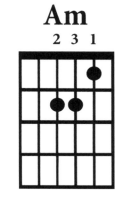

B
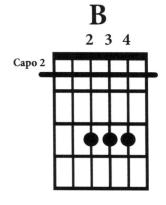

Bm
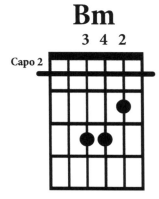

duviPlay

Basic 7th chords

C7
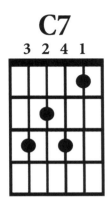

CMaj7
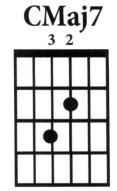

D7
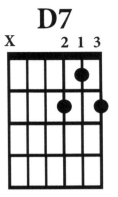

Dm7
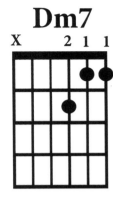

E7
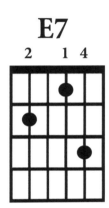

Em7
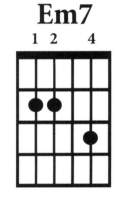

F7
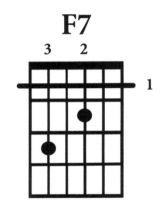

FMaj7
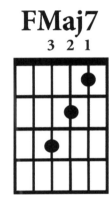

G7
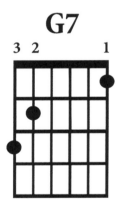

Gm7
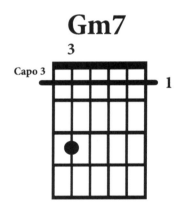

A7
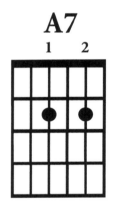

AMaj7
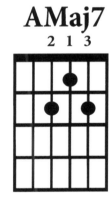

Am7
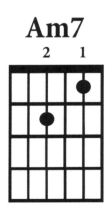

BMaj7
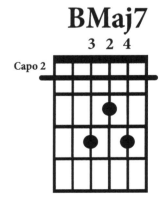

Bm7
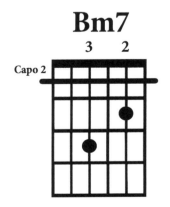

B7
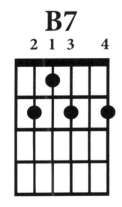

Collection compiled and transcribed by Tomeu Alcover
© Duviplay Music Publishing. 2017
www.duviplay.com
ISBN-13: 978-1977963406
ISBN-10: 1977963404

Made in the USA
Columbia, SC
12 March 2022

57575399R00041